Ship's Log

David Punter

Bristol Books CIC, The Courtyard,
Wraxall Hill, Wraxall, Bristol, BS48 1NA
www.bristolbooks.org

Ship's Log
Written and researched by David Punter

Published by Bristol Books 2022

ISBN: 9781909446335

Design: Joe Burt

A CIP record for this book is available from the British Library.

Introduction

THE SS GREAT BRITAIN is a ship, and an extraordinary one. She was designed and built in Bristol by the legendary Victorian engineer Isambard Kingdom Brunel, launched in 1843, and was the first large ocean-going ship to be built of iron and equipped with a screw propeller. From 1845 to 1854 she was in fact the largest passenger ship in the world. She had accommodation for a crew of 120, with a passenger complement of 360. She ran aground in Dundrum Bay, County Down, in 1846, but in 1852 she was repaired and subsequently sailed thousands of emigrants to Australia. In 1882 she was converted to all-sail, and three years later 'retired' to the Falkland Islands, where she was used as a warehouse, quarantine ship and coal hulk, until she was scuttled in 1937. In 1970, thanks to the generosity of a benefactor, she was raised, repaired, and towed back to the UK - itself a remarkable further feat of engineering - where she was returned to Bristol, where she has since been converted into an award-winning museum ship.

The museum has an attached archive, which contains many files of records. Some of these are diaries, letters and other accounts kept by people who travelled on the ship - mostly as passengers, but we also have the words written by crew members, ship's doctors and officers. I have been reading through these archives for several years, and have been continually startled by the extraordinary words in which those on board attempted to convey and craft their experiences, to form some kind of explicable narrative - to explain to others, but also in many cases to explain to themselves. In many cases, these would have been for those writing their first experiences of the sea; of the wonder and tumult, the ever-changing colour and ever-fluctuating shape, of the open ocean. They show evidence of some real wrestling with words, of trying to find ways to express the glories and terrors of a world hitherto foreign to most of the writers.

Stirred by this, I have attempted in this book to provide some response to the given accounts. I have done it by, first, reproducing some extracts from the records. I have changed these in only one way: I have altered the lineation, in order to highlight the poetic quality of some of the language used. Otherwise the words belong entirely to the writers - and I should say at this point that I am grateful to the Brunel Institute and Trust and to the SS Great Britain's staff members, particularly Mollie Bowen and Joanna Mathers, firstly, for providing me with help in accessing the archives, although they are of course freely available to any member of the public who cares to visit; and secondly, for granting me permission to reproduce the very words of these writers without running into any permission problems. Second, I have written poems which, in one sense or another, attempt to respond to the seafarers' preoccupations and articulations.

Of my poems, I have nothing further to say, except that some attempt to return to the historical world of the SS *Great Britain*, while others do not. Versions of a few of them have been previously published: 'Other Lives' appeared in *Literature Today*, and subsequently in my collection *Those Other Fields*; 'In Davey C's' in an earlier collection of mine, *Asleep at the Wheel*, as well as on a CD of my poems, *Flashes in the Dark*; 'Gull' in my collection *Stranger*, as well as on the CD of Echoes and Edges, a poetry and music collective of which I have been a part, *Glory in the Bone*; 'Albatross', under its alternate title 'Cormorant', also in Stranger; 'Ship-Shape', under its earlier title 'A General History of Mutiny', in *Scarlet Leaf Review*; 'Vulcan' in *Stranger*; and 'The Wreck' in *Line Breaks*. For some of the versions contained here, I have to record my thanks for advice received from fellow-members of two poetry groups, Bristol Stanza and The Lansdown Poets; and for creative weeks in Ger-y-Cwm, a cottage on Cardigan Bay, with friends Barry Hill, Liz Lumley-Smith and Sarah Parkinson as well as my wife Caroline.

Of the extracts, there is all too much to say, but it is difficult to express, and it is better left to the words to speak for themselves. Perhaps, though, the American painter Robert Henri put it well when he said:

We are tied to the ocean. And when we go back to the sea, whether it is to sail or to watch - we are going back from whence we came.

Whether that is the case or not, I hope that by reproducing these extracts I have given some sense of the ability - and need - of ordinary people to respond with articulacy and elegance to situations of the utmost strangeness, such as can only perhaps be experienced on the deep ocean; to experiences of raging tempest and blinding calm, of death and survival, of wonder and marvel, of seemingly impossible encounters with distant shores and inexplicable creatures. If I have given some renewed life to these words, preserved for us from over a century ago, then I will, I hope, have achieved something; and I hope the reader will prize and savour these words as much as I have.

D. P.

Contents

As we followed our southern course
the sea became tranquil,
and the manifold beauties of tropical days and nights gradually unfolded themselves -
days all gold and nights all silver.
Our ship spread her white wings
and sailed slowly and gracefully
over the foam-flecked, sparkling waves.

(excerpt from Frances Isabella Dukerley, *Campaigning Experiences in Rajpootana and Central India*, Cork to Bombay 1857)

Colours of the Sea

Like a tropical dream
like an imagining of luxury and treasure
like a manifold that can no longer, or never again,
be re-folded, hidden under the gown, the robe,

                sea swirl, deep channel, midnight sonata

because the robe has been spread,
like a net to catch the heavens
or a net of stars,
an endless constellation where

                zephyr, cat's cradle, wind chill

what is above matches, invigorates, incandesces
that which is below
and a great chain of being rises upwards from the ship's wake
bearing with it souls, spirits, beings of grace,

                stolen sapphire, blue nuthatch, stardust highway

and the mere sparkling transmutes into a finer
realm, where we are transcended, transcendent,
the concerns, the fears of the voyage
left behind as we imagine the very pure.

                faded indigo, paradise found, blown glass

Three days before our arrival at Bombay,
a gloom fell upon us, owing to the death
of one of the men of the 17th Lancers ...
at five o'clock the following morning he expired,
and was buried between ten and eleven o\clock
the same day.
The quiet of the calm and shining sea
robbed his grave of its horror.

(excerpt from Frances Isabella Dukerley, *Campaigning Experiences in Rajpootana and Central India*, Cork to Bombay 1857)

Quietus

We think of death as horror
we are possessed by the gloom of the grave
from birth to death the shadow falls upon us
but then again, and again, there is the sea.

The ocean knows nothing of these things -
yes of course, the ordinary horrors
happen without abatement
shark eat lesser fish, crabs seize,
jelly-fish perfect their venomous art.

But there is also a quiet
which is not only a quiet of hearing but also a quietus,
a making of peace before the end
where times mean nothing
except that, always, it is in the dark
that the real ceremonies occur.

Another calm day. Here and there in patches
there is a ripple on the water ...
the water being perfectly smooth gives it
the appearance of a river winding through a flat country.
The track of the ship was traceable
for miles almost to the horizon.
I sat for some hours on the cross yard
reading Oliver Twist
and whilst there saw a large whale
at about a quarter of a mile from the ship ...

(excerpt from the diary of Samuel Archer MRCS, Cork to Bombay 1857)

Twist

Oh, the joy of this miraculous moment! I too want
to rush at Oliver, at the publication date (must have been
quite recent) but perhaps it does not matter - in the writing
of life there are always ragged-footed urchins,
nowhere more than at sea, where anybody could end up
press-ganged, chained, all these myths about
life as a cabin boy, the excitement, the abuse,

but how, I want to ask, how did this well-fed passenger
get permission to climb to the cross yard?
And how is it that all these passengers have a mysterious
grasp of nautical language - or is it deeply inbred?
Is there something in Britain's nautical soul
that constantly requires myths of the sea,
angels with salt-scarred faces climbing the shrouds,

always ill-fed, always lured onwards by wild promises
of whales, dolphins, porpoises, many miles
away from the terror of the poorhouse, the bowl
of ill-conditioned gruel, always the victim as hero,
the twist in the tale, fear and horror reinscribed
as wonder and enchantment, the shanties and ballads
reimagining the pain of the endless turning of the capstan,

unending nights cowering beneath the lurching deck?

After the sun had gone down
a sort of pale yellowish white sky was left
above the horizon
fading with the deep blue ... In a short time
the sky changed into a most delicate pink
or rather violet which faded on either side
with blue and the yellowish sky ...
In the pink floated light gray clouds. ...
the tint [is] indescribably delicate ...
[We] anchored about half a mile from the little town.
As we steamed in
we knocked off our foretopmast sternsail boom
against an American ship.

(excerpt from the diary of Samuel Archer MRCS, Cork to Bombay 1857)

Crafting the Language

All the sweet colours of creation
float about us now; and they challenge too.
How shall we find, or craft, a language for
the indescribable?

         Were we to float away,
engaged on our strange poetic voyage,
how would we retain eyes to see,
to observe that which is before our very eyes,
another ship, all too close, full of hazard,

how would we see the little town
where the antique mariner finally comes to port,
anxious lest his sea-legs desert him,
staggering through the streets searching
for another inn,

         a place to rest between
the endless journeyings, a place too to find
another recipient of the immortal story,
the tale of the beautiful sailor lad
hired to satisfy a rich man's wife

and fill her dreaming eyes with the narrative
of the sea, where all things that happen
fall from the mind, dissolve in the myriad spaces,
glisten white upon water?

Numbers of fish about the vessel.
We saw a large black creature
walking along the bottom of the sea
which we supposed was a turtle.
It was about four feet long and nearly as many broad.

(excerpt from the diary of Samuel Archer MRCS, Cork to Bombay 1857)

Depths

Ah, the creatures of the depths,
how they constantly amaze,
dimly glimpsed

through the perils of parallax,
full of legs, like slimy things
that walk the slimy seas

awaiting benediction,
transformation into coral,
achievement of a shaped body

that we can recognise,
clarify with a name
so that they no longer resemble

the many shapes of death,
the fear of what might lie
at the bottom of the sea,

childhood terrors
of crayfish and squid,
seaweed draped unwelcomely

over our infant toes
or a crab placed by malicious hands
in the hood of my anorak,

and me screaming
as I feel the tiny pinch of pincers
struggling to be free,

and do not understand
the terror of the creature itself
torn from its native habitat.

... we put off to the ship under canvas.
The water was brilliantly luminous,
the stars shone brightly and every now and then
a flash of light like the reflection of a white cloud on the water
shot from the sides of the boat
as we startled a shoal of fish.
The lights of the town behind us
and the indistinct outline
of the great mountain rising above it
formed a beautiful picture the vessels
with lights in the windows before us.

(excerpt from the diary of Samuel Archer MRCS, Cork to Bombay 1857)

Under Canvas

A small boat darting across the sparkling waters
    illuminated by the lights of home
reminds us of the beauties of the sea's strange daughters
    with hair of silver and with teeth of foam.

Conrad's captain's hat bobbing on the tide
    directing us to the safety of a lee shore
reminds us that when we stare over the side
    eyes agape cannot glimpse the ocean's floor.

The mountain looms, we recognise the land
    with all its practices, stratagems, essays
as something foreign, ill-sorted, in the hand
    of gods who know nothing of the sea's deranging ways.

The sea will save us all, we hope, or drown us
    absolving guilt and fear, the fatal twins,
and wrapping its wild bounty all around us
    in a sleep that knows no errors and no sins.

Like illumination in the manuscript of life
    it throws the earthly into black and white
cutting strange pictures with a sea-blue knife
    into the pages with a lover's gentle bite.

We learn to dwell upon the wine-dark ocean
    with all the skills that memory bestows
and it rewards us with its own devotion
    mute hints of all it loves and all it knows.

There were a few other animals I think Selpae
floating about. There is a very minute animal
which I have several times noticed
in the tropical seas
moving about on the surface of the water
like a small water beetle
or a fly trying to get out of a bowl of milk.
I cannot at all see its form
but merely the commotion it makes.
Expect to get into Bombay on Thursday next.

(excerpt from the diary of Samuel Archer MRCS, Cork to Bombay 1857)

Selpae

Selpae: *asleep, elapse, please,* all you get
of this creaturely life afloat or adrift
are re-formations, but they too make a kind of sense:

these tiny creatures, too minute to see may indeed
be *asleep* until disturbed by the attentions of the naturalist,
and as he watches, alert for the merest movement,

the slightest indication of purpose, motive, motion -
will he notice time *elapse* as, transfixed as on a pin
and constant in his endeavour to match, to find

similarity, to invent new sea-borne metaphor,
he fails to notice the slipping away, the hiatus
in mind as he is possessed by this new sense of being,

by these creatures who appear to do exactly,
confidently, with commotion, unintelligibly
even to these marvellously adapted senses of man,

whatever it is they innocently, indolently, *please*?

The heaviest sea we have had yet
breaking over the bows
to the great amusement of some
and thorough drenching of others.
Wind fell during the night
a good deal of lightning from the East,
this is the first day I have felt afraid. ...
A whale seen at a distance
spouting up water, dancing on the quarter deck
from 8 till 10 o'clock. A woman in the Intermediate
lost last night. £5 - 3 which was made up
today by subscription.

(excerpts from the diary of an unknown passenger,
Liverpool to Melbourne 1863)

Lost Last Night

The first day and the last night
        heavy seas
               and a terrible death
      described all too briefly
         felt by none
compensated by mere money
              as though pieces of silver
        could be somehow converted
                into that other silver
         of the ship's wake
where her body is left behind
            unhouseled unannealed
      prey to the depths
              while we dance like water-flies
      on a surface so flimsy
that all of our delight becomes necessary
              as a counterweight
       to that first flush of fear
the realisation that we float grimly
         atop the wild realm
that has always reminded us
      of return abjuration
         the abandonment of a life
     which comes to appear
             a mere flight of fancy
a frail construction over the abyss
whence we sprang unarmed
       to confront circumstances
           never of our own making
which seem even to include
      a whale
     spouting at a distance
       an impossible miracle of being
to which we can never come too close.

Shipped a heavy sea today
which dashed in upon the Captain's state room
and drenched him completely,
it broke down into the third cabin
and filled it to a depth of 3 feet.
At 4 o'clock a heavy lurch again
when the fore stuns'l boom dipped into a wave
the sail caught the water which filled it and
snapped the yard arm like a piece of glass …
it created a stir for the time. …
Bible class in the evening
which was very largely attended
by both old and young
and was very interesting.

(excerpts from the diary of an unknown passenger,
Liverpool to Melbourne 1863)

The Ark Adrift

Heavy sea
      heavy lurch
            piece of glass

Heart of glass
      breaking like a chandelier
            on the Titanic

A stir for the time
      a stir in time
            whirlpool of glass

Bibles on shelves
      swept away
            the ark adrift

Old and young
      brothers together
            perhaps sisters too

We dash in
      full of hope
            and stare at the spectacle

The Third Cabin
      drenched and afloat
            Save us Lord

Fearfully cold with occasional heavy showers
of hail, wind much lighter and the sea presenting much the appearance
of an infuriated goose pond. ...
all sails clued up which gives the ship
a lonely bare and wrecked appearance,
I having been so long accustomed
to see her in full dress.

(excerpt from the diary of an unknown passenger,
Liverpool to Melbourne 1863)

In Full Dress

Perhaps if we can persuade ourselves
that all this turbulence, this spectacle of majesty
is but the village green writ large;

perhaps if we might restfully suppose
that the might of ocean
is being seen through the wrong end of a telescope;

perhaps if we can cheer ourselves with the thought
that hail never lasts long, and is always gone
in the coming of the bright and hopeful morning;

perhaps then we can banish the Nightmare Life-in-Death
in her ship with rotted sails on a windless sea
and dress her again in a frail but glowing finery.

Knocked about from 4 in the morning
till 6 in the evening when the weather changed
immediately a cry of Land
on the port bow when to our joy
we discovered the Australian coast in the distance
with Cafe Otway lighthouse,
our ship hoisted her signals
to which the lighthouse replied by rockets,
our ship then shot up four
which had a beautiful effect
falling like stars.

(excerpt from the diary of an unknown passenger,
Liverpool to Melbourne 1863)

Fireworks

The fireworks start: huge gold chrysanthemums
paper the sky. The startled valley hums
with wine and water. On the farther bank
torches scurry. We are dwarfed by the mountain's flank.

Black beams, red ceilings, upper rooms aglow
we protect ourselves with the leaping sounding show,
imagination's gleams. The river spits
green fire. Through the tautened crowd there flits

a momentary spectre, soon allayed;
the signs are all too confidently displayed.
Along the road, fear takes a different form;
fairground neon disguises the coming storm.

Foie gras country; live geese with golden beaks
await the hoops. An endless organ creaks.
The special swagger moves through every aisle
where thwarted snipers find their longed-for style.

Unmarked trucks circle the blaze; the night
prowls. Forms hover and loom in the rifle's sight,
presaging crescendo. As dodgems spin and clash
and children's arms clutch candy, goldfish, trash,

the war of emblems takes a grander turn:
we watch the trails of emerald rockets burn
and evaporate. Hills move a footfall closer.
Under the awnings, village baker and grocer

opine that, this time, the fires will never die;
a final spectacle opens, sears the sky.
The sound dies. Then, as excited chatter begins,
foot-shuffling, shaking of overcoats, proud grins,

another sound comes. Over our heads, behind,
the mountain starts to echo. Rock-plates grind.

Sitting down on my chair the other day
I broke the bottom right out
so have sent it to the joiner
to be mended tonight. ...
The wind had entirely ceased
and the sea appeared
as one immense piece of custard pudding.

(excerpts from the journal supposedly kept by Edward Mills Grace,
Liverpool to Melbourne 1863)

Trades

The Ship's Carpenter

Shipshape, they say, and what is shape
but this fine holding together of cross-trees,
strake, each fitting perfectly into the other
so that the minutest of cracks, the tiniest of trickles
is sufficient to raise the hairs of my head
as I sit dreaming, with a mouthful of nails.

The Ship's Sailmaker

They billow and slap, their edges rough
and painful to the touch, and will not lie down
despite my most delicate of ministrations;
needle and thread, needle and thread, I am reminded
all the time of my cosy tailor's shop in Bristol
before they came with their shilling and their drum.

The Ship's Cook

'While she floats, I shall cook' - so goes the old saying,
as he served up coffee to sailors sitting on yards
and beams all out of true on the hull-wreck -
but the real danger is scalding, they say most ships' cooks
have the staggers and shakes, but as they eat
their hearty breakfasts they do not stop to think why.

The Captain's Steward

A fine gentleman indeed, with his full dress and sword,
and always polite to me when I bring his meat and coffee
which I dare not touch; but only I have seen him
spread-eagled and shaking, vomiting up last night's
tasty supper, cursing the day that he was born, the day
he signed the gilt-edged papers; but I do not say a word.

Last evening a child about 5 years old
died of dysentery so they sewed him up
in canvass and tied a cannon ball
to his feet and tossed him overboard
at 1/2 past 2 in the morning,
but not before the minister
had read the burial service over him.
I think I must get introduced
to some of the ladies
to simply pass the time away.

(excerpt from the journal supposedly kept by Edward Mills Grace,
Liverpool to Melbourne 1863)

Children of the Sea

What, after all, is it to me? I never
meant this voyage, and as to why they sent
me off, why, that is the business of no one
except my own.
        Let me just say there was
malignity afoot, none of it done
of my own making.
        One or two of the servants
turned out to see me off from the morning house,
standing nervously under the yellow portico
in rain; my Mama and Papa, the earl,
conspicuous by their absence.
        And no sign,
of course, of Elizabeth or of her blasted brother.

A voyage is good, they say, for ripe beginning
to make a new life; but I am sunk in memories
of home, of my childhood; and so it is I wonder,
who was this child - I know I never saw him
but I have seen others, crumpled steerage children
with grimy faces and even grimier clothing.

Did his Mama love him? Perhaps she did,
perhaps even now she is flooded, racked with tears
in her sun-blistered, seasick compartment -
but I cannot think of that; I find I need
companionship, not salt thoughts of the dead;
wine not seawater, and a pleasant grateful maiden
to while away the roiling ebbing time.

When we got on deck after dinner
the sky presented a most beautiful appearance.
It looked all over
if you had taken a nice soft paint brush
and just touched it all over,
or as if a sudden gust of wind had come
and scattered it into a thousand little bits. ...
[The sun] had for exactly half the circle
a beautiful tint of scarlet
gradually dying away
into nothing but blue sky ...

(excerpt from the journal supposedly kept by Edward Mills Grace,
Liverpool to Melbourne 1863)

Seastruck

how to describe the edge that is no edge
or the shading of the ineffable, where words fail
and my senses reel, all thought forgotten
or erased as if by the strokes of a child's
paintbrush dappled in God's palette

what lies behind this blue enormity
the ship and all those on it
mere actors on a fully accoutred stage
under the all-seeing eye of heaven
a golden haze, a yet more golden wake

and this will be so for these many mornings
as we glide untroubled through the mazy deep
and the very thought of land recedes
behind the creak of tackle, the gust of sail
the roar of a mighty engine beneath our feet

I am entranced, bewildered, my withers wrung
sunk in humility, all my compass points
soaked and reversed, sea and sky upside down
sea-locked, water-cleansed, washed by a draught
of angels and their blue seraphic wings

Today the vessel rolled a great deal
and one of the fore shinsail booms
dipped into the water and got broken …
The main yard weighs eleven tons
and is 105 feet long.
With the shinsails it is 165 feet long
that is from end to end.
The weight of the yard on the main mast alone
is over 30 tons, that is without reckoning
the weight of the mast itself. …
My gathering gets worse
likewise the boil on my nose
right at the end of the proboscis.

(excerpts from the journal supposedly kept by Edward Mills Grace,
Liverpool to Melbourne 1863)

Of Yards, Booms and Shins

Shinsail: no such term to be found in nautical dictionaries; could be
an error for sprit sail, which would be flown below the jib, although
attachment to the main yard suggests something quite different

Boom: a pole which controls the position of a sail (whether existent,
misnamed or neither); a deep violent sound, sometimes produced by the
unending clash between waves and ships' timbers; a floating barrier of
timber across river or harbour mouth, constituting hazard

Yard: a long beam on a mast for spreading square sails, almost certainly
not involved with shin sails or sprit sails, but the length of which sailors
needed to clamber atop the rocking ocean; a ship-building establishment

Main yard: principal such beam; or yard extending over the main,
sometimes for a considerable distance (for how many yards? what distance
over the main, the open sea? how far must sailors travel from the ship's
side, never looking down?)

105/165 feet long: therefore each 'shin sail' (assuming they exist and there
are two [how did this passenger acquire his specialised vocabulary?]) must
need an extra 30 feet (10 yards) of yard; and these are yards, remember,
that must be travelled by the sailor setting sail

Shin: the front part of the vertebrate leg below the knee (essential for men
shinning up the rigging), otherwise known as 'shank' or 'crus' (from Latin
crus for leg, not to be confused with 'crux' [Latin *crux* for cross, the shape
of the mast (main, fore or mizzen) with its attendant yards])

Boil: a painful gathering, not unlike that of men after a shipmate has been
washed overboard, perhaps in a boiling sea, where the waves may threaten
to swamp those unlucky enough to be caught out (on the yards)

Proboscis: a trunk or long snout, not usually used to refer to the human
nose, protruding beyond the mouth though only rarely protruding beyond
the end or flanks of the ship; when afflicted with a boil, a sore cross (or
crux) to bear ...

23 is Mr Humphries 22 years
who is a very nice fellow.

24 is a young fellow from Scotland named Burns about 19.
He will come to no good
being too fond of drinking.
25 is Mrs Hopkins who has been ill
and not able to come to meals since we started.
26 is Mr Hopkins a Liverpool merchant.

27 is a funny little hunchbacked German
named Shokarkt. He is in some business
over in Geelong. 28 is Mr Hodgson
An money lender at Ballarat
who has been home to England
to marry an old maid.

(excerpts from the journal supposedly kept by Edward Mills Grace,
Liverpool to Melbourne 1863)

Other Lives

Wondering about those other lives
Is the beginning; a small start,
A flicker of light, the harassed
Mother in the train carriage,
Trying to handle Samsonite
And pushchair all at once.

And then you think (though maybe
It's a detour, this) that
Really there are no other minds
At all, just blocks of flesh
That move and mouth and have
A being none can fathom.

But now this child has begun
To cry, and you can see
So clearly what's required;
While fathoms deep another
Voice responds, inside
Yourself, or from another

Place entirely, where
Antique sympathies strain
For our always distracted
Attention. Haltingly
The light grows stronger.
We cannot help but know.

43 is Mrs Moore a pretty good sort
only you want to follow her
with a coal scuttle and broom
to pick up all the Hs she drops.

(excerpt from the journal supposedly kept by Edward Mills Grace,
Liverpool to Melbourne 1863)

Mrs Moore

If 43 is Mrs Moore
I wonder who is 44?
And when they gather on the deck
Will they all say 'Flippin' 'eck'

And 'oover up the tea and cake
Or raise old 'ell with beer and steak
While dancin' tangos in the bar
Goin' tearful over Ma and Pa

They're 'eaded for Austral-i-a
Expectin' bacchanal-i-a
And all that will fulfil their 'opes -
In Britain they've been on the ropes

But Mrs Moore is on the ball
She isn't fazed by class at all
Although she's only down in steerage
She 'obnobs with the rich - and peerage -

She 'its the bottle every night
Recoverin' before daylight
While envious souls around 'er swirl
Pronouncin' 'er a game old girl.

5th verse:

Some advice may I give the purser good fellow
The owners I fear are not so bright as their name
Let us have on the table port & sherry more mellow
That we may drink his good health in a glass of the same
Now fill me a bumper of the best liquor on board here
A toast I'll propose now join me who may
Here's success to the Great Britain and all that is in here
And three hearty cheers for Captain John Grey.

End

We saw a lot of porpoises
close to the vessel this evening.
They were about 6 or 8 feet long,
white and brown,
very large stripes.
The screw went down again this evening.
My finger a good deal better today.

(excerpt from the journal supposedly kept by Edwards Mills Grace, Liverpool
to Melbourne 1863; song composed by Mr Moore for a ship's concert)

In Davey C's

In Davey C's, between Yonge and Bay, south
of the parking lots surrounding the Chelsea Inn,
faces swim in the gloom. Forkfuls of rich
hors d'oeuvres and pastries tango, a silvery sheen
glistens and throbs. The music is submarine,
a smiling of teeth and scales. Clear green water,
Hawaiian, resplendent with turtles, laps the sills;
the Ramone punks by the bar walls gape; great trays
of seafood rise and dip on the swell. Cocktails
of pomegranate and oyster overflow the glass.
Beautiful whitening bones litter the floor.
The chef wears a king-crab helmet. Nothing perturbs
the roll of this rudderless ocean. Take me along
to high tide hour, sinking in Davey C's.

The ship rolled and laboured so much
that I expected the mainmast to go every minute,
the lanyards of the topmast backstays
gone on both sides
and several of the main rigging gone.
What with the ship rolling and shipping so much water
it was impossible to save others.
While doing so one man fell overboard and was drowned
as we could not render him
any assistance. ...
I had a most anxious time of it,
I can assure you,
and wished that I had never seen the Great Britain.

(excerpts from a letter by Henry Stap [captain] to his brother,
Liverpool to San Francisco 1882)

The Storm-Spirit

I thought my last dull breath was gone that night
as lightning flashed and ropes entangled wove
a grim tormented pattern on the deep
and all the longed-for life for which I strove
seemed fair undone in welter of the brine.

There rose before me shapes I did not know
slipping from poop to fo'c's'le in a trice
a moving shadow-show of all my life
upended by a fell throw of the dice
and naught for comfort on the thrashing main.

Death stalked the cabins, swept the heaving decks,
and God (my God!) was nowhere to be seen
as water flowed in rivulets so pale
across the pale face of the ocean's queen
to whom I had entrusted this my life.

The trim concerns of land all fell away
between the screams and shouts of those who swayed
along uncoiling hawsers 'tween the yards
and those below who only clenched and prayed
for deliverance from night's unending wrath.

Amid this tumult I espied a ghost
staggering seaward between the anchor-chains
bearing a gale-tossed body with my face
and then I knew that my sad groans and pains
meant nothing to the mockery of the deep.

I can never forget the scene -
there was tragedy too -
a sailor, in endeavouring to furl part of a sail on the main yard
that had been blown loose
lost his footing and,
after hanging on to the bellying canvas for a few seconds,
fell, striking full across the iron railing of the gangway.
I can see the first mate now - a burly fellow -
slinging the dead man, like a bag of flour, across his shoulder
and taking him below.
Luckily the gale abated and we ran into beautiful fine weather
but just off Madeira we met with disaster.
We were bowling along before the wind
with every available stitch of canvas & studding sail booms outrigged
when, just before break of day, we ran into an American barque. ...
Our main yard was in a very dangerous state
and might fall any minute so volunteers were called
to go out to the end to make fast some tackle.
Another exciting incident occurred -
the sailor had just got out to the very end of the yard
when it parted in the middle, coming down crack on the bulwarks,
but before it touched, the sailor sprang into the sea
and, as we were under steam at the time,
was soon a long way astern.
However, he was a Liverpool diver by trade and a good swimmer
and to the delight of everyone was picked up safely.

(excerpt from 'The Greyhound of the Deep', a letter by
Arthur Anthony Robinson, Liverpool to Melbourne 1858)

The Black Pearl

You Liverpool divers, you good fellows all,
should never forget the tale I'll unfurl
whether you're serving on tanker or yawl
thinking of home or your mother or girl

As the seas bound across and the great waves uncurl
and the solid iron parts like a sheet of tinfoil
and you're caught in the rigging and sent for a whirl
mid the Kraken's foul stench and Leviathan's coil

Whatever the rocks mighty ocean may hurl
to make a man blench and his face deadly pale
there's always the luck of the price of a pearl
to think on when braving the jump from the rail.

Wednesday arrived at St Vincent,
letters on shore and went there ourselves.
Had jolly fun seeing the blacks running about some of them 'A la nature'
we saw the English burial ground & the English consul.
What a rum place it is.
I shouldn't like to live here not for any money.
Got Surtees on shore, the 4th best billiard player in England,
according to his own statement
& beat him, proving for the 4th time that he was a boasting ass.
Some Scotchmen, Paddies and the like went on shore
& got so jolly drunk that they began a fighting among themselves
& several were brought on shore half dead, that was all.

(transcript of an account given by John Selby Walker,
Liverpool to Melbourne 1858)

Rum

(n) A spirit distilled from various products of the sugar-cane, and prepared chiefly in the West Indies and Guiana.

> *to be found on shore, with disastrous consequences for some*

(n) The name has also been improperly applied to spirits made in imitation of this from beetroots and other materials.

> *perhaps this was the problem;*
> *Scotchmen and Paddies can't be trusted to tell the difference*

(n) Used generally as a hostile name for intoxicating liquors.

> *are the natives hostile? am I hostile to the natives?*
> *or to Scotchmen, Paddies and the like?*

(n) A poor country clergyman in Ireland.

> *or thus referred to, at any rate, by Mr Swift,*
> *not noted for his civility to the out of the ordinary*

(n) An old or unsaleable book.

> *or any other reject, surviving beyond the pale of civilisation and elegance*

(adj) Good, fine, excellent; great.

> *as in Surtees' boastful self-assessment,*
> *perhaps produced under the influence of rum*

(adj) Odd, strange, queer.

> *as in the behaviour of others when they do not conform to our expectations*

(v) To cheat.

> *But that was not, of course, how I beat England's 4th-best billiard player*

Saturday night's row.
A great many of the passengers having been well charged with drink,
which they got from the bar
(where we are privileged with French brandy, Old Jamaica Rum (good)
and wine at 3/- and Ale and Porter at 1/- per bottle)
about 11 o'clock got fightable;
but in order to quell any disturbance Captain Grey very prudently interfered to stop it,
but was quickly hit, knocked down and trampled on.
The 1st Officer then came to his assistance with sword in hand,
bawling loudly to his fellow officers to come and assist him,
and swearing that he would run the first man through who offered any resistance,
he then with his fellow officers released the Captain
from the grasp of the assailing mob,
and after awhile again restored peace,
after first taking the principal ring-leaders (some 2 or 3 men) into custody
and confining them in irons.
But in consequence of the numbers who still loitered about the decks,
and gathered in groups for a considerable time,
the Officers fearful of any further outbreak, released them,
after being some 2 or 3 hours in confinement.
Matt and I thought best to keep out of it, by going to bed.
Fortunately there was no mischief done.

(excerpt from the diary of William Bray,
Liverpool to Melbourne and Sydney 1854)

Our Sad Captain

All this is hard to stand - the need for speed,
to outrun the competition, and all the time
the entitled passengers, drunken with complaint,
blind to the ocean's glory, only bent
on their own status, when full half of them
are here because of their own unowned misdeed.

I walk the rail alone, and try to see:
the money's been good, my Uist family
is safe from the factor's foul predation,
ignominy of poorhouse; would abandoning my station
mean that this vast housing of mystery,
these impossible engines, would turn better without me?

The devil take the sea. I'll pay my bill
and have no more truck with the running dog
whose only thought is for blue commercial flow.
The time has come, while the others drink below
in lounge or wardroom, to try conclusions in the fog:
and let posterity make of it what it will.

for Captain Grey, lost at sea, 1872

This day we had beautiful weather but very little wind
and we had the screw down the whole day.
There is a good deal of swell for we are off the Bay of Biscay
and we roll very considerably in consequence.
The phosphorescence in the evening was magnificent finer than I had ever seen it before.
The numbers of large luminous medusa was very great
and a track of white light interspersed with balls of greenish hue
extended a considerable distance from the stern. ...
Saw today for the first time a Portuguese man of war.
It was of a beautiful blue colour edged with pink
and a membranous sail rose from the body above the water below the surface
of which the remainder of the animal was visible.

(excerpts from the diary of Samuel Archer MRCS,
Liverpool to Melbourne 1857)

Medusa

... a man hears what he wants to hear/
And disregards the rest (Paul Simon)

You have tried to blacken my name down the unrolling centuries
    accusing me of violence
        of a terrible blinding

When I was weaponless and you came at me with sword and shield
    and all I did was throw back to you
        images of your own destitution

My hair was black and gold then and now it is grey and silver
    and yes it writhes as women's hair always writhes
        in the eye of the beholder

My offences, you said, were multiple: unattached, childless
    bound only into a fatal sorority, incarnation of anima
        menacing the true gods.

Stheno, Euryale, they knew my weakness, knew I could be killed
    mourned and wept the bitter tears of women's wisdom
        the wide world over.

You always want to cut hair, an offence to patriarchal order,
    but your medicines are snake-oil, your jolly barbarity
        reeks of the locker-room.

I had the power to freeze men's blood, it's true; but only when that blood
    ran hot and fierce in the worship and joy of battle
        killing my kind.

Snake-hips, tentacles, a cold and soaking embrace even to the point of death -
    all these are your fantasies, your cloud of sexual unknowing,
        your elaborate fear.

Shall I sit here on a rock, combing my long languid locks, mistaken for a mermaid,
    or shall I imitate your ways, vow vengeance, scorch your eyes
        with all you refuse to see?

The southern cross which has been visible for some time
is becoming daily brighter
and we now have the benefit of a full moon.
This evening we had a beautiful sunset
and afterwards one of the stokers played the Scotch Pipes for us
and we had a dance on the deck. ...
Today we have seen a new gull, 'the whale bird',
which is apparently about the size of our own gulls in England.
The back and wings is a puce colour and the breast white.

(excerpts from the diary of Samuel Archer MRCS,
Liverpool to Melbourne 1857)

Gull

We've got 'em bang to rights, the noisy screamers
and harbingers of our oceanic discontent;
Jonathan Livingston, George Barker, Chekhov,
fish and chips, snatched sandwiches, a certain
stink of half-remembered, half-digested fish.

Forgetting how huge they are is one thing; worse
is forgetting how *gull* they are, how unlike
anything else in the many wild kingdoms we
pompously incline to regard as our home despite
the anarchy of mosquito, buzzard, lynx.

A white head endangered among rocks, scrabbling
claws spread to meet the gust, there is nothing
romantic about this unseasoned life, bare feed
and guano, profitless, enduring, cold
as midnight, we think, is cold; but always cold.

In moments we are gull, instances of dream,
flapping from the black precipice, swooning
in the down-draught, knowing no knowledge
except the squawking mouths, the endless need
revealed for a second in cowl of black and grey.

The albatrosses are becoming more numerous
and with these and in larger numbers is the mollyhawk
a large brown gull
almost as large as the albatrosses themselves.
It is most interesting to watch the birds skimming over the water
all but touching it with the tips of their wings
and then soaring high in the air
or wheeling off to a distance suspiciously
when any thing is thrown overboard
they all flock together
and it is then that the enormous size of the albatross is most apparent. ...
They reminded me very frequently of the restored pterodactyl
in the Crystal Palace Gardens.

(excerpt from the diary of William Archer MRCS,.
Liverpool to Melbourne 1857)

Albatross

The harbour is studded with small floats –
plastic containers, cans, anything that will

hold an orange rope. I walk past
as a small boy points over my shoulder

asking his father, 'What's that?'
'An albatross'. An albatross?

I swing round in amazement and see
nothing, to begin with. Then,

perched on a floating pink beach ball,
spectral black, wings outstretched,

elegantly keeping balance,
not an albatross. A cormorant.

Have I been the victim of a joke,
or seen a vision? How to choose ...

Cormorant

Today one of the passengers died of inflammation of the Lungs
and he was buried in the afternoon.
The body was sewn up in a piece of canvas
with some lumps of iron to sink it
and then covered with the union jack
was carried by six sailors in their best dress to the lee gangway
and the burial service having been read by Mr Taylor
the board on which the body was placed
was tilted up on end
and plunged into the sea.

(excerpt from the diary of William Archer MRCS,
Liverpool to Melbourne 1857)

Ship-Shape

top
rigging
(it's all rigged)
chance game
twixt decks
of hands
but now at the top-gallant furling out strong winds
sweating swearing
in press
gang-way
of companions
cap'n swings
(will swing)
down below
in fire
eternal
with the padre's
bowl of lemons
as we heave
mainbracing (the mainsail) our yard-arms angle at 70 degrees
above the swell
of ocean
widow-maker
but a captain
(as the capstan turns)
will be widowed
in his many-windowed
poop cabin
tonight
will taste of the sea make his pleasant reconciliation
with the fathers of oak and sea-green teak
all ship-shape (what is the shape
of a ship as it dwindles
down to nothing
below the
keel)

Regular bands or ribands of light
of a beautiful greenish hue
floated past in considerable numbers.
Looking over the stern we could tell when one was coming
from the flash of light which preceded it
and long after we had passed them
we could see them shining brilliantly.
I fancy they are something like the Certum Veneris of the Mediterranean. ...
My poor larks do not seem to flourish very well and several of them have died.
I hope however to get some of them safe to the end of the journey.

(excerpts from the diary of Samuel Archer MRCS,
Liverpool to Melbourne 1857)

Excess

It is all too much,
    far too much.
        My senses cannot withstand

this constant barrage
    of the unexpected, the all too
    beautiful.

And the deathly;
    why is it that I have to be
    confronted with these

wild excesses which proceed
    so far beyond
        my capacities?

Yes, my larks have died
    (and very sorry I am for it)
    but here are strangers:

Sea-creatures and birds
    a-plenty, nothing in common
    with my poor larks

nor with any other known
    being in the realm of God
    and in a way it is a relief

that the poor fellow dying
    (I did not know him)
    comes to remind us

that all is not so strange;
    that death is to all of us
    our last friend

on this unreadable ocean
    where beauty masks
    the shapes of fear.

... at present we have every day
seen something Fresh in the Sea -
Ships Flying Fish Birds Porpoises
and for the first time Grampuses were seen today -
I have been on Deck the whole day
and in the evening I was there looking at an old Friend
with whom we must soon part perhaps for ever
(this is a solemn Thought)
I allude to the Polar Star but his brightness
is already getting dim and we are looking forward to
the new and shining Constellation of the Southern Cross.
This is the last visible link almost
to the Northern Hemisphere
but there are still many bright and shining Stars
which to me will never grow dim
however much their brightness may be overshadowed
by the New Constellations
and there is also another thought which gives much consolation
it is that these northern or southern Friends or Stars
are not 'Fixed Stars' but that there is a centre of attraction
to which they will sooner or later fly.
Oh what a joyful meeting will that be -
where there will be no more separation
and where all will sing the praises of the Great Ruler of all Events -
oh let not any of our Happy Family be absent at that joyful meeting.

(excerpt from the journal of Robert Saddington, Liverpool to Sydney 1853)

The Resurrection of the Grampus

And will I be included?
I know not what I am.
I seem to have a horn,
but I cannot separate myself
from the ocean floor.

I huff and puff, it seems,
but how can this be
if I am made all of water
and flow through your imaginings
in shapes beyond conception.

You have made me in an image
as God, you claim, made you
in his; but who or what
is my prototype, where is
the cave that holds my form?

I long to be as one,
but I am all of scattered parts,
through books, records, fears
of what the great waters may hold.
Perhaps I am all wrong.

Will this wrong be righted?
Will I attain a state of grace
where all the curious creatures
nosing through the abyss
will be recognised for their own?

I transubstantiate;
I twirl, I giggle, and I watch
your scared incomprehension
while longing to be as one,
with you, with life, with God.

The sea was running very high all night
and rolled us about in our berths.
I slept until 4 o'clock when I was suddenly aroused
by water running down my face,
so I got out of bed and lighted a candle. ...
I dressed and went on deck: it was a beautiful sight.
I had never seen the sea in its splendour before.
The waves were truly grand and the ship, under full sail,
was bravely cutting over them at 14 nots [sic] per hour,
braving the billows most gallantly. ...
Only 3 or 4 including the officer on watch,
were on her vast decks
which all day long are crowded with hundreds of human beings.
This led one to reflect.
I thought of the 800 people beneath, quietly asleep.
I thought of the number of hearts beating
in the bowels of this mighty ship
and that, like a large town so deserted at night,
in a few hours would pour forth her teeming population
to their daily employment - and occupation.
I thought what a frightful scene it would present
if a fire were to break out.

(excerpts from the diary of Olcher Fedden,
Liverpool to Melbourne and Sydney 1852)

Vulcan

At his old tricks again, spitting lava
Down the sleep of the innocent mountain,
Rearing skyward, the sun disappearing
Behind the bars and lattices of the night.

Or roaring 'Fire Down Below'
As the mainmast's rigging crashes in flame
And the magazine splits its sides
In the torrential laughter of the burning.

Or the flamethrower slashing
A body in two as the walls cave in
And scorched blocks collapse
In the city where nothing stands.

First he kept the wolves at bay,
Then warmed the cooking-pots, gave the family
A hearth of affection, guarded against
The storm's bitterness and woe.

Then we found him better uses,
Turned him to tasks of division –
What is born of the flame shall perish
Of the flame, and not be healed.

Janus the two-faced is pallid
Beside these flickering images
Lit by fire, dying by candlelight, of
Vulcan, always rearing at the back of the cave.

I had retired to my berth a little before nine,
fatigued with the anxieties of the day,
but was still awake to observe every stage of the disaster.
My first premonition of it was a succession of unusual motions,
at intervals of half a second, quivering and creaking
through the mighty framework of iron,
like the convulsions of nature in an earthquake.
This was soon followed by a tumult above,
which convinced me that disaster of some sort impended,
and I rose and dressed myself with all possible speed.
I ran upon deck, when, lo!, the misty outlines
of an unknown coast were visible through the darkness,
from which two lights reflected a fitful glare of blue flame
to our anxious view - land so beautiful, so delightful,
under ordinary circumstances, now revealed itself to us,
perhaps, with its shelving rocks and its quicksands,
as a ghastly spectre to menace calamities the most fearful,
the talisman of a speedy and a fearful death.

(letter of Rev. Pharcellus Church to *The Dublin Christian Record*,
Dundrum Bay 1846)

The Wreck

At high tide, the tips of the masts are visible;
as the water recedes, they are canted, booms
and crossbars describing impossible angles;
the decks remain below, unseen, saturated.

I move on down, through the grey and blue,
rusted capstans, the gleam of rotting cannon,
rolling casks that have ended in the scuppers,
the ship's cook endlessly relighting galley fires.

The crew gathers around me, signing wordlessly
to avoid the rocks; but the helmsman
is dead at the wheel, lolling in his chains
and today's rum ration will be forever preserved.

Flood seeps up the hold companionway;
there have been horses here, tethered in stables,
and a cargo of ore and loose timber
which would have rolled free upon catastrophe.

A mute cabin boy shimmers in the darkness,
hair tousled, clothing disarrayed, a letter unwritten
to a mother who will never cease from waiting,
from calling his name into the oceanic void.

The sea-creatures phosphoresce in the gloom,
their blind gaze illuminating emptiness as I stare
at coil upon coil of rope, vast rectangles of canvas,
six-inch needles and thread in the sailmaker's workshop.

'I was a tailor on Cheapside', he whispers, 'until
the king's men came, and my clothing was fine';
but then there were shin-sails and top-gallants to patch,
and shrouds to fashion as homage to the widow-maker.

Swimming upward past the captain's cabin,
an elegant scene unfolds, all scarlet and rosewood,
empanelled cupboards, ornate windows - stove in now
where starfish and the great eels make their kingdom.

Breaking the surface, clinging to a disintegrating spar,
I look out on the vast acres of swell and feel the tug
downward, ever downward, where vessel and man
are one in the push and pull of death's dominion.

... *strapped to the mast,*
I could observe without terror the spectacle before me.
The scene was superbly grand
as the storm king rode triumphantly over the mighty deep
and drove the foaming billows into little mountains
which when they met each other in mighty fury
would throw their white spray high into the air
then sweep over the deck.
Now we go way down into a valley
between those mighty waves;
I look fore and aft; the foaming sea is far above us;
we are lifted by the monster wave to the crest of the water,
the big heavy ship plunges her prow straight into the next mountain approaching;
her steel beams vibrate and resist firmly
the onslaught of this most severe test of her strength. ...
The sea continues rough and squally;
the ship rolls very bad;
it sends us from one side to the other with a vengeance. ...
It is quite chilly;
most of the passengers crawled into their berths to keep warm.
(We wonder if they now envied the strong faith
of the despised Mormon missionaries?)

(excerpts from the diary of Thomas Steed, London to Melbourne 1875)

The Mormon Missionary

There is no chance of sleep.
Below, in Third Class, I can hear the fighting
among the ones who only live to tope
and prevent me from Writing.

I live to spread the word.
I am despised. I hear the voices howl.
Life's lessons are learned best when they're learned hard;
spit in my breakfast bowl.

I lived among the blest;
God and the Prophet sent me on my way
amid the heathen, the rigging and the blast
to hail another day.

There are three nuns aboard -
no doubt on a mission similar to mine,
except their well is poisonous, rank, deplored
by the great will divine.

I shiver and I retch
but God is with me through the dreadful night
and the Great Angel; I shall then be full rich
When I am in Thy sight.

Creaking timbers warn
all night of the weight of mighty flooding seas
but I prevail; I know I was not born
to drink the bitter lees.

Last night I spoke to one
who fain would be converted; but he was sick,
all other hope had fled this haunted man
and I would not play a trick.

When I come to the coast
of that land where they roil in heathen revel
then shall I truly break my holy fast;
unman the threat'ning devil.

We were anxious to say prayers for the emigrants
but could not for some time.
However we went among them,
exhorted them to keep quiet,
as some of the patriotic ones went about throwing down the preacher,
so it is a wonder some trouble did not result from it -
they hold out for the 'Holy Ladies',
and when some Protestant population of 3rd class and steerage
passed some cutting remarks on our dress
Paddy at once took up our cause,
and threatened to strangle the offenders.
We promised them articles of devotion
and hope to make them more civilized before we part from them. ...
After lunch we said our office of the dead entire.

(excerpts from the diary of Mother Mary Paul Mulquin,
Liverpool to Melbourne 1873)

Civilisation

prayer   emigration
exhortation   quiet
patriotism   preaching
holy   ladies
population   steerage
cutting   dress
Paddy   offenders
strangling   devotion
civilisation   dead
office   lunch

Civilisation, we might say, is the quelling of violence/the granting of respect to other religions/other beliefs/an exhortation to quieten the impulse to strangle or to throw down/to refrain from cutting the dress or the address/ to pay all our dues to the dead and the recently dying/the seasick and those bamboozled by devotional paraphernalia/to make space for a quiet office lunch even when feelings and seas/especially seas/run high/to give voice and ear to the emigrant/the immigrant/to those of all places or none at all/ to whole displaced populations moving about on the high seas under their own will or not/moved by the impulse of adventure/by patriotism/or by need/those who preach and those who endure preaching/those protected by the holiness of their calling or unprotected against the prejudices of the multitude/it is a means of making ends meet/of bringing together without the sharp edges of spars and anchor chains/of making the most of a watery element which promises to rub away the thorns and pricks of life/while all the while also promising an unseen office of the dead which will be read over us even while we are still trying to read the signs/the signs of an incipient violence or the signs of an endlessly deferred landfall when all our sins will be accounted for and the dead will be counted/those who have perished amid the perils of the sea/those for whom the only words/preached incessantly over the rolling waves/the roiling tombs/will be/as the seas run high and stained with the blood of the emigrant/'Hail Mary full of grace'.

Not long after
the water made its way through the portholes
inundating the berths under them -
the sufferers were Mother Bernard and Mother Patrick,
both of whom sleep under the windows.
It was a laughable sight
to see Mother Patrick jump out of her berth
exclaiming 'We are drowned'
and then lying down on the floor with a blanket round her -
the rule of silence cannot be strictly observed here,
even after night prayers,
there she lay calling our attention to the stars ...

(excerpt from the diary of Mother Mary Paul Mulquin,
Liverpool to Melbourne 1873)

Suffering, Sleep, Silence, Stars

I really thought the end was nigh
I'd feared it all my suffering life
feared it in the midst of prayers
when sins whipped through me like a knife

I'd longed for sleep, but sleep came ill
with dreams of sickness in the field
the field where I had lived my days
before I took God as my shield

I cannot know what is to come
when I arrive on heathen shore
what silence will astound me there -
will words avail me never more?

But here as I am brushed with death
astonishment o'erwhelms my soul
the stars are many, the stars are free
they flood my mind from pole to pole

The comedy the body makes
when severed from its usual place
swoons before this sublimity
as I see God's work face to face

I roll, I tumble and I laugh
at the edges of this grand design
and I am soaked, amused, distraught -
but stars hang clear upon the vine.

Breeze still fresh
ship going 14 to 15 knots an hour
heavy sea on.
Tremendous fighting again last night in our cabin
& great excitement again today
owing to all the 2nd, 3rd and 4th cabin passengers
having an allowance of grog served out to them with Dinner,
such a row about a drop of rum,
when will men know better.
None of our mess had any we were all teetotallers.
There was one man who tried to throw himself overboard
and nearly succeeded in his purpose,
this afternoon carried away fore lower stunsail
& broke away the main top gallant sail,
but they got it secured again,
the sea is running mountains
& the ship rolls fearfully at times,
some noise with boxes and tins.
Got great noise & fighting again tonight.

(excerpt from the diary of Walter Edmonds, Liverpool to Melbourne 1873)

Rickety Rackety

Everything is rickety rackety they are brawling and
upsetting the furniture such as it is with their shenanigans and
nothing on this ship is stable or firm the sails blown away and
even human life is no longer to be taken for granted and
my metaphors fail me in the face of these sea-mountains and
I no longer know which way up I am there is no-one to dress me and
the words spill out over the bunks and spoiled bedding and
I think of the old farm spread so evenly before the sun and
even now I cannot concentrate for they are swirling through the door and
my balance is gone I have no sea-legs nor any legs at all and
I have never been a great dancer but

                        perhaps this rickety rackety
is what dancing is like and if I ever get to Australia alive
it might be good to engage in a little more of it unless of course
it conduces to falling over and making a fool of myself but
that might be a price to be paid for a newer freer life.

So much wind today have
to take in some sail very
cold & plenty of snow on
deck to day some of the
passengers making snow-
balls & bringing in the saloon
for the ladies to look at
walking on deck difficult
& very high sea crashing
over us occasionally as if it
was going to swallow us up

(transcript from the diary of an unknown passenger,
perhaps John Brooke, Liverpool to Melbourne 1869)

High Sea

And as the sea is deep
and my curled fingers frame
an avalanche of you

and my heart stoops
to pluck you from the snow
of many journeys

all but concluded
within the glass of years
there will be a ball

and all will bow and sway
as on a great ship
sequestered and boundless

moving with the rhythms
of oceans all a-boil
the giant mother-god

of pearls and estuaries
snow-lakes unconfined
melting before the mast

turning a ghostly capstan
it will never be the same
again and again bar rock

and sea-spoil from which
may we be forever protected
elevated widow-maker

Star of the Sea hostel
for the drenched abandoned
and my homecoming

to you not swallowed yet
in these difficult seas
that never obscure
a snow-pure remembrance.

Notes to the Poems

P. 11 - all the colour names mentioned on the right of the page are drawn from a contemporary domestic paint chart.

P. 15 - Dickens' *Oliver Twist* was actually first published in book form in 1838

P. 17 - the reference to 'the immortal story' is to Orson Welles' wonderful film of that name, released in 1968 and based on a short story by Karen Blixen, writing under her pen-name Isak Dinesen, in *Anecdotes of Destiny* (1958)

P. 21 - the 'captain's hat' and its behaviour is a major feature of the ending of Conrad's novella *The Secret Sharer* (1910).

P. 23 - 'selpae', it appears, is now spelled 'salpae'; a salpa is, according to the Collaborative International Dictionary, a kind of 'transparent, tubular, free-swimming oceanic tunicate found abundantly in all the warmer latitudes'.

P. 25 - the last part of the extract is ambiguous: 'lost' could refer to loss at a game of chance, but in such a case it is difficult to see why other passengers should feel obliged to 'compensate'. I have preferred to suppose that 'lost' is a euphemism for 'died', and the amount of money referred to has been raised to be passed to the deceased's nearest and dearest.

P. 29 - the 'Nightmare Life-in-Death', who 'thicks man's blood with cold', figures in Coleridge's 'The Ancient Mariner', first published in 1798.

P. 33 - this poem, like some of the others in *Ship's Log*, is partly anachronistic; it seems to suggest that the ship's sailmaker, for example, has been forcibly pressed into service. This, of course, was a practice only used by the Royal Navy, and it ended in 1814, although it was not made illegal until some decades later.

P. 45 - 'In Davey C's' is set in Toronto in the 1980s.

P. 49 - this poem is based on 'Liverpool Judies', a well-known capstan shanty.

P. 53 - 'to try conclusions' occurs in *Hamlet*, Act 3, scene 4, in the course of one of Hamlet's unpleasant upbraidings of his mother Gertrude.

P. 57 - the three seagull references are to the 1973 film *Jonathan Livingston Seagull*, directed by Hall Bartlett and adapted from the eponymous novella by Richard Bach; George Barker's novel *The Dead Seagull* (1951); and Chekhov's play *The Seagull*, first produced in 1896.

P. 61 - 'Captain Swing' was actually the presiding genius of the labouring men who rioted in 1830 in protest at low wages and increasingly expensive goods. This may seem remote from the sea, but in fact the dire economic situation had been worsening ever since the sudden demobilisation of soldiers and sailors at the end of the Napoleonic Wars. See Eric Hobsbawm and George Rudé, *Captain Swing* (1969).

P. 65 - it is now accepted that 'grampus' is another name for various perfectly real species of dolphin and killer whale; but the name also has a long and distinguished history in the other world of sea-monsters and demons.

P. 67 - 'Fire Down Below' has a history as a sea shanty, and has become a common phrase with a multitude of meanings extending well beyond the nautical; it is also the title of a number of modern songs and films. There is a wonderfully eccentric and suggestive rendition of it by Nick Cave on *Rogue's Gallery: Pirate Ballads, Sea Songs, and Chanteys* (2006).

P. 69 - some aspects of this imagined ship, perhaps especially the horses in stables, are modelled on the SS Great Britain.

P. 79 - The 'widow-maker' has been a common epithet for the sea from at least the 1590s; Star of the Sea, Stella Maris, is another name for the Virgin Mary, patron saint of mariners.